1001 Arabian Nights at the
Burj Al Arab

ABC Millenium

Copyright (C) 2000
Khuan Chew and Uschi Schmitt

First published in Cyprus
by ABC Millenium.

Second Edition February 2003
Third Edition October 2005

This book is edited and designed
by Khuan Chew and Uschi Schmitt.

Printed and bound in Italy.

ISBN 9963-621-71-6

This book is dedicated to

**HH Sheikh Mohammed bin Rashid Al Maktoum
Crown Prince of Dubai and UAE Minister of Defence**

with gratitude

CONTENTS:

INTRODUCTION

No expense in terms of imagination or creativity has been spared in the design and construction of the Burj Al Arab. It is a symbol of Emirian ambition. Its destiny is to become not only one of the great hotels of the Middle East but the world.

For a hotel to be compared with magnificent icons like the Eiffel Tower, the Burj Al Arab is a structure that has evoked strong opinions and emotions. This was the result of a very evocative brief.

The Brief

The challenge was put to **architect Tom Wright** of **WS Atkins** in 1993. The brief was to design a state of the art, futuristic building. It had to be Arabic, extravagant and super-luxurious, and would become a symbol for Dubai.

A dream project for any architect, the realisation of which took more than 150 WS Atkins architects and engineers, a 40 strong **interior design team (KCA International)**, over 4000 construction staff on site **(Al Habtoor Murray & Roberts; Depa Arabtec)** and countless other contractors, suppliers and manufacturers, local and international, working side by side.

The Approach & Concept

Tom Wright's approach for the architecture of the Burj Al Arab was to seize on Dubai's historical seafaring tradition. However, instead of borrowing the time-honoured shape of a dhow sail, he fine-tuned the design to incorporate the profile of a modern, high-tech yacht sail, taking design and technology forward into the next millennium.

At 321 metres tall it is truly giant and is currently the 15th tallest building in the world in addition to being the tallest single structure standing on a man made island. Set 290 metres off-shore (in order to avoid placing the Jumeirah Beach Hotel and the Wild Wadi Aquapark in it's shadow) its unique shape now stands out amongst famous world structures and has become an icon for Dubai.

For inspiration, **Khuan Chew** of **KCA International** looked to the land, its people and their culture. From the harsh terrain of the desert with the scorching summer sun beating down to the austere mountains of Ras Al Khaimah. These images belong to a people who have an innate understanding and respect for the natural elements of their land that has been their homeland throughout history.

The Emirians have progressed from their nomadic roots to become a country with one of the highest per capita incomes in the world.

To celebrate their forward thinking and achievements in history despite the harsh environment, the Burj Al Arab was to encapsulate the affluent society that now exists.

The interior is a showcase in palatial proportions with combinations of rich colours based on Earth, Air, Fire and Water.

The desert was a canvas onto which was painted a palette of explosive colours depicting the four elements.

In designing the Burj Al Arab, one had to have an understanding of the Location; it's culture, people, climate and future. Equally important is Arab hospitality, which is recognisably second to none. In Arabic tradition, each visitor to one's home should be received and welcomed as if he or she was a manifestation of the Prophet.

In its recent times, the older generations can still recall the nomadic Bedouin tribes that roamed the stark desert, graciously offering food and shelter to passing caravans. Here at the Burj Al Arab, this tradition is being followed by its 'seven star' service, the envy of hotels the world over.

T H E   F O U R   E L E M E N T S

CONCLUSION

The new generation in the Emirates today, like any other, relates to a world of designer goods and ultra modern edifices.

The **Burj Al Arab** is a balance of east and west, old and new, oriental and occidental, the modern and the traditional. The design is a successful result in meeting the needs of a broadbased market right through the spectrum.

From the ornate opulence of traditional Arab interiors to the very modern, ultra-slick clean lined interiors, the Burj Al Arab contains a room to satisfy every taste.

THE TEAM

The design and construction team recognised that no one person nor company can excel in all areas and that allowed each component of the team to make meaningful contribution to the ultimate benefit of the project.

This included the major role played by the hotel operator **Jumeirah International** who evolved the operational requirements of the brief, during the onset of the design programme.

This book is a record of how "we saw and did it". Although we had never previously designed anything of this scale, we rose to the challenge to produce one of the finest hotels that the world has ever seen.

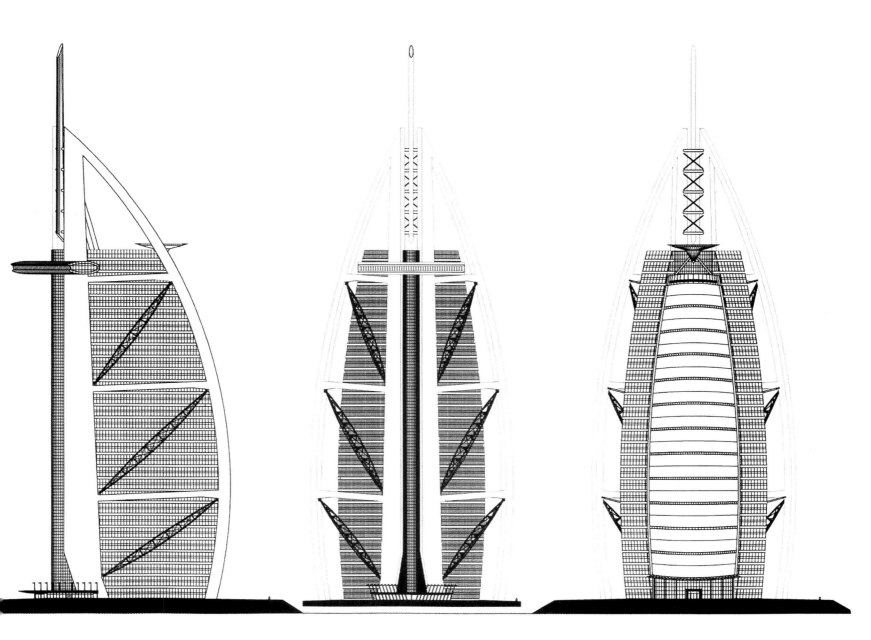

DESIGN OF MAIN STRUCTURE

The unique shape of a modern yacht sail is recognisable miles away upon approach.

Standing 321 metres high, the Burj Al Arab is the tallest stand-alone hotel structure in the world. It is built on a man made island 290 metres out to sea and linked to the mainland by a slender, gently curving road bridge.

The island is protected at its base by special hollow concrete armour units which are perforated and slopes to the sea thus providing the absorption and protection from the impact of the surrounding sea waves.

The Burj Al Arab is built on sand, which is unusual as most tall buildings are founded on rock. Supported on 250 columns 1.5 metres in size, 45 metres under the sea, the columns rely on friction as there is only sand to hold the building up. The diagonal trusses (largest is 85 metres) on the side of the building are as long as a football pitch and weigh as much as 20 double-decker busses (165 tons).

Built in Dubai 15 km away, they were brought by road on 80 wheel lorries specially imported. The highest truss took a day to lift into. Engineered to sway a maximum of 300 mm at the top based on an average (in 50 years) 45 mps/mph, the total volume of concrete in the superstructure is 36,000 sq. metres.

An architectural and engineering excellence for the 15th tallest building in the world. The mainly in-situ concrete structure is triangular on plan, with exposed diagonal steel wind bracing. The structure holds 28 double height floors (56 storeys) measuring 7 metres floor to floor, with a helipad at a height of 212 metres above the sea, a 60 metre mast at the top and a cantilevered restaurant 27 metres long on the 27th floor (200 metres above sea level).

Total size of Burj Al Arab in plan gross area 1.2 million sq. ft.

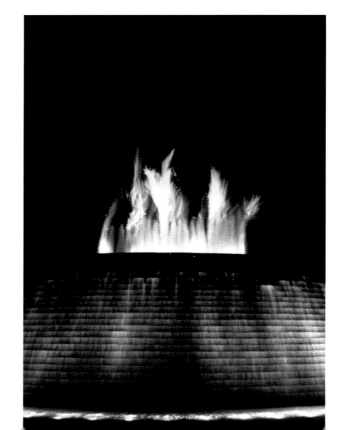

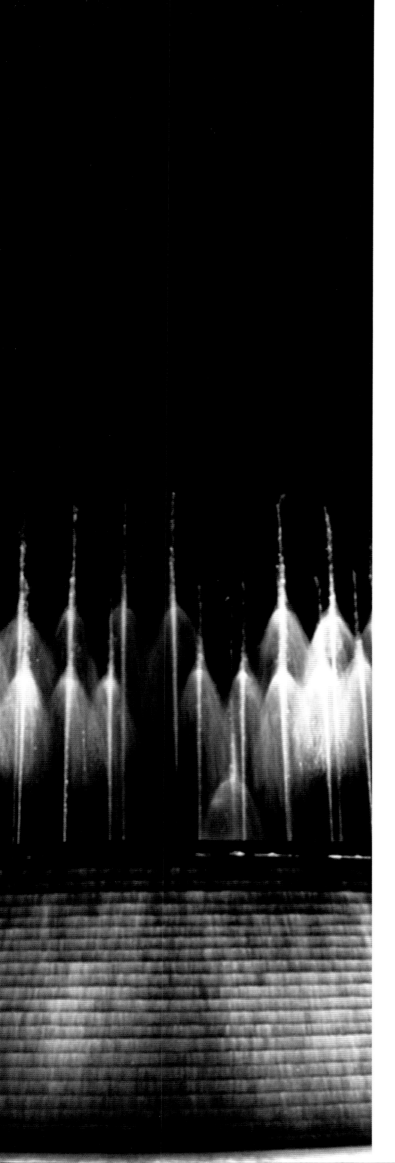

EXTERNAL FIRE & WATER FEATURES

The external fire and water features are associated with the arrival experience starting at the approach bridge across to the man made island site of the Burj Al Arab.

The concept is comprised of 2 major components: 2 pairs of monumental fire towers frame a "gateway" into the arrival court, offering spatial definition to the space, and an elliptical cascade element centred in the vehicular loop, incorporating a variety of exciting water, fire and lighting displays.

The fire towers are abstract, architectural forms that work in concert each half-hour to produce a rhythmic pattern of powerful rising spherical balls of burning flame.

The central ellipse is set in an elegant circular blue granite pool. Overflowing water sparkles white in the sunlight as it skips down the stepped slope of its granite walls. The perimeter of the top of the cascade is dressed in a tightly spaced ring of kinetic jets - MicroShooters®. The core of the plan is occupied by a cluster of MiniShooters®. These are powerful water jets capable of achieving great height. Running through the long axis of the ellipse, addressing both the hotel and the bridge are a row of WETFire® nozzles.

These intermingling water and fire displays are totally new and exciting centrepiece in the design. All of these richly choreographic displays are internally illuminated in white and coloured lights at night.

ENTRANCE LOBBY

The Entrance Lobby of the Burj Al Arab is an elliptical shape outlined on the floor by the thickest hand tufted carpet in motifs of the 4 Elements with a reflected ceiling coffer in gold framing a glass and mirrored chandelier, flanked by two gold circular shells specially cast in GRG finished in gold dust.

2 escalators aside giant size Aquariums with the most exotic tropical sea water fish link the Entrance to the spectacular Atrium, the tallest in the world.

ATRIUM

The atrium is 182 metres high (596 ft.) with a volume of over 285,000 cubic metres. Try to imagine the Statue of Liberty fitting quite comfortably inside. It is the stage for a multitude of engaging features - Feast your eyes with an explosion of intensive rainbow colours on every floor, tropical fish aquariums, a water cascade on tiered beds of coloured glass, gold painted gigantic columns, multi-patterned coloured mosaics on the floor, a water sculpture, psychedelic lighting effects on the fabric sail wall.

CASCADE WATER FEATURE AND AQUARIA

One ascends the atrium via escalators on either side of the Water Cascade up to the First Floor. The spectacular 'waterfall' gently descends down diamond tiers of coloured glass aggregate where 24 pairs of coloured fibre optic lit water jets (Leapfrogs®) dance in programmed sequence, and causes a "fire spark" when they collide and form a stimulating light show. From all angles and heights, the Cascade Water Feature creates exciting visual patterns according to the choreographed computer programme day and night. The Wind element is portrayed by dry ice, programmed to emit mist which carefully descends down the water cascade.

FIRST FLOOR WATER BASIN FEATURE

The focus of the First Floor level is another Water Feature - a circular basin filled with sloped trays of coloured glass aggregate from which spring 24 white fibre optically lit water arches (Leapfrogs®) and a perimeter of 6 "MiniShooters"® of Water Jets surrounding the main "HyperShooter"®, a powerful but controlled water jet column that can be projected up to a maximum height of 50 metres into the Atrium space.

Timed to perfection (like the finale in a musical symphony) at the end of the "clapping" dance rhythm of the Leapfrogs and "MiniShooters", the HyperShooter is a spectacle in itself well worth the wait!

Water motif in floor mosaic

ATRIUM FABRIC WALL

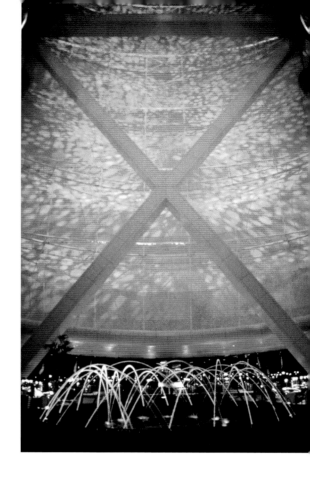

The solution to overcome the complex 3 dimensional shape of the hotel atrium wall whilst maintaining the overall sail-like form of the building was to provide a series of shaped membrane panels that could be patterned to the defined geometry. The membrane is constructed of PTFE coated fibreglass separated by an air gap of approximately 500 mm and pre-tensioned over a series of trussed arches. These arches span up to 50 metres between the outer bedroom wings of the hotel which frame the Atrium, and are aligned with the vertical geometry of the building. The double - curved membrane panels are able to take positive wind pressures by spanning from truss to truss and negative wind pressures by spanning sideways.

The trussed arches which can extend out from the supports by up to 13 metres are supported vertically at the 18th and 26th floors by a series of 52mm diameter cross-braced macaloy bars. Girders at these floors transfer the load to the core structures. The macaloy bars are anchored at level 1 to a substantial entrance girder which is tied to the lower basement structure. These bars are then pre-tensioned to ensure that the whole structure remains in tension.

The properties of the fabric makes it appropriate for the Middle East region where its predicted lifespan and self-cleansing qualities should resist the aggressive environment. The fabric also reduces solar gain into the atrium and provides an effective diffused light quality during the day. At night, the Atrium Wall takes the place of a backdrop canvas for a spectacular light show of a myriad of projected colours and patterns internally and externally.

Total area of fabric : 8,700 square metres

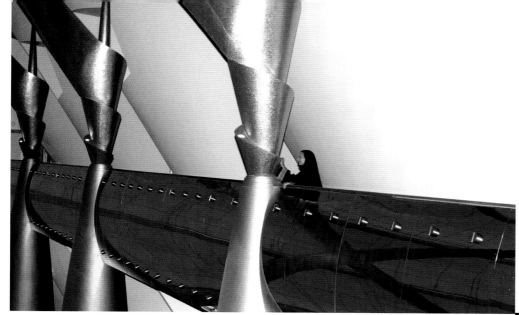

GRP Sail Wall

The Sail Wall was built up as a Composite Panel made up of 3 mm GRP (glass-fibre reinforced polyester) with inherent fire retardency, 25 mm Polypropylene fire retardant Honeycomb, 3 mm GRP, 60 mm Rockwool with density 180 kg/m3 and 1 mm GRP (fire retardant) inner protective skin.

It is the largest GRP construction (m2) ever awarded and the first time GRP/Honeycomb has been used as a Fire Wall. It is also the first time GRP/Honeycomb forms the only load bearing structure in a panel of such a size (average panel measures about 110 m2 and is 14 metres long and 8.5 metres high with returns), weighing 3.5 tons each.

VIP ENTRANCE

A separate VIP entrance with lounge & private elevator for special guests on the Entry Level.

SAHN EDDAR
Atrium Lounge

The Sahn Eddar which seats 120 on the first floor of the Atrium is THE meeting place, an oasis for light refreshments, a voluminous but relaxing lounge framed by 10 metre gold columns. A first class lounge to experience the magical water feature performances, gaze at the tallest and most colourful Atrium in the world, and enjoy the amazing light show on the fabric sail wall.

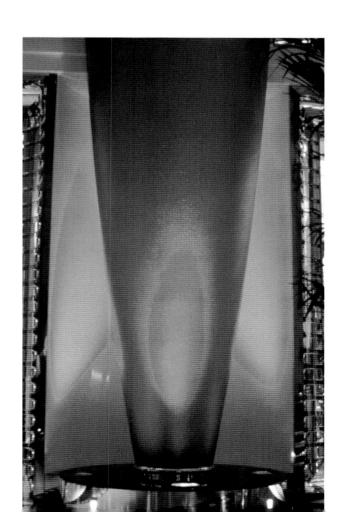

AL IWAN

The Al Iwan, on the first floor off the Atrium, is the Middle Eastern and International Cuisine restaurant with a capacity of 110 covers. Divided into 3 intimate but adjoining dining areas, it is adorned in colours of Crimson Reds, Black, White and Gold.

The Al Iwan is richly finished in glass mosaics, gold leafed arabesque arches, cherrywood carved panels, gold on red printed fabrics, traditionally inspired flame-glow wall lamps, with finishing touches of carefully chosen objets d'art in hand made Venetian glass, and oriental artifacts of gold and black lacquer.

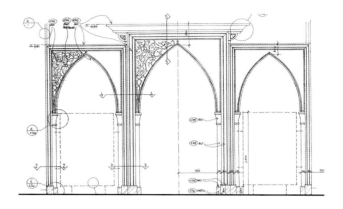

JUNA ("Eye of the Sun")
Cigar Bar

On the mezzanine floor, and its worth finding it, the Juna's cocktail bar lounge is a sumptuous and most comfortable intimate 35 seater drawing room richly furnished in warm tones of gold, yellow, black and red.

A hideaway place to watch the sun set or enjoy a cigar and a drink with friends and other guests late into the wee hours of the morning.

LIFT LOBBIES

Titanium plated steel Architraves, mimicking the bulge lines of the external fabric sail wall, frame the elevator doors in the Lift Lobbies.

6 guest lifts travel at speeds of 7 metres per second (16 mph) to all floors and 2 Wall Climbers (Panoramic Lifts) travelling non-stop at 5 metres per second (11 mph) to the Al Muntaha Restaurant on the 27th Floor.

AL MAHARA ("The Shell")
Seafood Restaurant

Travel in style in a capsule, and experience a memorable 3-minute simulated submarine ride with wrecks and marine life on the way, into the depths of the deep sea restaurant of the Al Mahara. Arrival point of the capsule 60 ft. below sea level is the Wine Cellar leading through a gold arched shell tunnel into the main Aquarium restaurant. An exotic array of thousands of tropical fish of every colour and hue dart among coral in the central elliptical shaped Aquarium. An additional 3 Private Dining Rooms (the Addura, Shazra and Yara) with their own private aquariums of a total 1,000 cubic metres of sea water and fish in the Al Mahara.

Vertical fins back-lit in the spine from floor to ceiling divide the cast silver panels of waves on one wall. The theme of the Al Mahara is inspired by marine life such as coral, oyster, abalone and pearl reflected in the carpet designs, mother of pearl inlay in the furniture, and specially designed light pendants.

BAB AL YAM ("The Sea's Door")
Pool Terrace Cafe Restaurant

The Burj Al Arab's very private outdoor pool with its own jacuzzi is serviced by its own informal cafe, the Bab Al Yam. Dine inside or on the terrace deck with spectacular views all around.

AL MUNTAHA ("The Ultimate")
Skyview Restaurant
& Cocktail Bar Lounge.

Reaching for the sky on the 27th Floor, the futuristic Al Muntaha is seemingly suspended in mid-air. It is cantilevered 25 metres from the main structure and is suspended at a staggering 200 metres above the Arabian Gulf. Ascend via an express glass lift at 6 metres a second and arrive in a polished chrome and stainless steel space station lobby of the Al Muntaha.

2 tunnels in high tech "circuit panel" walls left and right leads into the Cocktail Bar and Lounge (seats 74) with a stage for live music and a dance floor, and the main restaurant, a fine dining for 140 covers offering the finest European and Mediterranean cuisine. Unbeatable magnificent panoramic views of Dubai and beyond from all 3 facades.

A contemporary design in a contemporary space, reflecting the 21st century in a space-age theme.

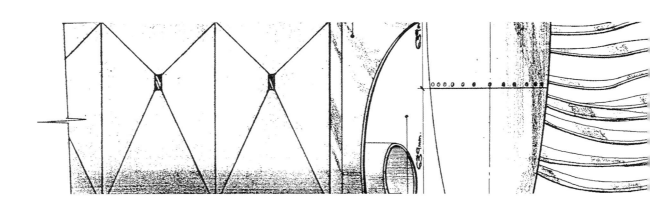

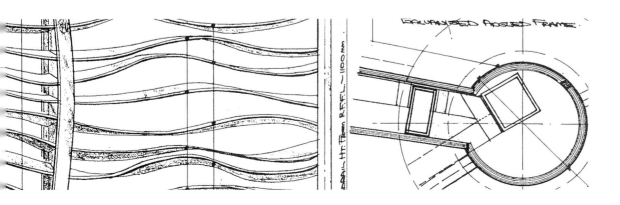

AL FALAK
Ballroom

Up on the 27th floor is the Al Falak Ballroom, a 2 tiered circular wedding cake decoration of golden yellow, pinks, oranges with black, brass and gold-leafed trims and accents, crowned with a gold leafed dome 11,140 metres in diameter, from which hangs a massive Swarovski Strass Crystal chandelier. It has a seating capacity for 220 and cocktails for up to 400. A Palatial room in its detail decoration of relief plaster wall panels, marblelised columns with their carved and gilt column capitals and the plush 100% wool hand tufted carpets make this one of the grandest formal spaces in the world.

AL FALAK
Conferences Suites

The Conference Suites of the Suheil, Suha, Athuraya and the Majlis Rooms of the Tameen and Al-Areeka are linked to the Ballroom via the upper tier of the Ballroom. A venue for the most special of events - be it a State Function, an International Convention, or ideal for a very private and exclusive celebration.

The very latest in computer technology and communication systems, dimmer control lighting sets have been installed in every suite to suit business meetings and conferences of the 21st century.

ASSAWAN
SPA and Health Club

Up on the 18th overlooking the Atrium is the Assawan Spa, the Arabic themed Spa and Health Club with 2 indoor Pools 1 Female "Katr Enada", one Mixed "Ma'Sama", endless treament rooms of the Yasmyna, Mesk, Allaylac, etc., jacuzzis, and a Gym with the latest equipment and qualified personal trainers. It remains open 24 hours.

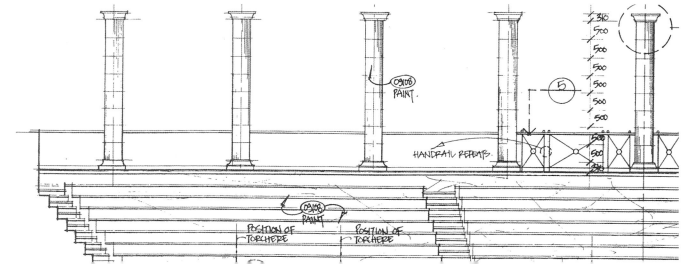

The amphitheatre lounge that joins the Male and Female Spa wings overlooks the dramatic atrium, a view that incorporates the Arabic Facade on the 18th and 19th floors, and the gigantic fabric sail wall, the canvas upon which light shows commence at dusk and run through in to the night.

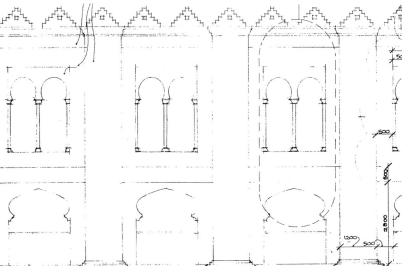

Inspired by the famous traditional Arabic and Turkish baths, the sumptuous combination of blue, gold and glass mosaics and colourful ceramic tiles, the 2 tranquil indoor pools overlook the sea and Dubai.

DIWANIA

Adjacent to the Health Club is a separate gentleman's club, the Diwania - Assawan Library, Snooker Room and Bar, exclusive to hotel guests only.

THE SUITES

There are no hotel rooms, only Suites. All little gems and precious stones of emerald, ruby, aquamarine, pearl, lapiz colours amidst the earthy metals of brass, silver and gold. There are the rarest of granites, Azul Bahia from Brazil, exquisite yellow marble Giallo Sienna (from only 2 quarries in the world in Northern Italy) and the now obsolete Fantastico Arni from a marble quarry that had been closed for 50 years (we knocked on their doors) and the lavish usage of Statutario White in all the bathrooms, from the same quarry as Michelangelo selected for his sculptures.

All bedrooms have spectacular views. The finest Irish linen adorn all beds and bedside controls provide pre-set lighting scenes. A remote control in this area activates the curtains and television. A dedicated bar is also located in every bedroom.

The Bathroom is floored with the whitest of Statutario White Marble, the shower floor and bathroom walls in reds and blues of Sicis glass mosaic from Italy framing the "window" mural of the Emirates above the circular whirlpool spa bathtub.

Specially commissioned, the mural depicting the familiar landmarks of the Emirates is the work of the young talented artist Jonathan Mason Stewardson who spent many months on research and sketching landmarks in the U.A.E.

The shower is installed with wall mounted body jets, with all gold plated bathroom fittings specially ordered from France.

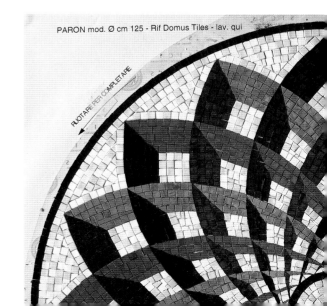

PARON mod. Ø cm 125 - Rif Domus Tiles - lav. qui

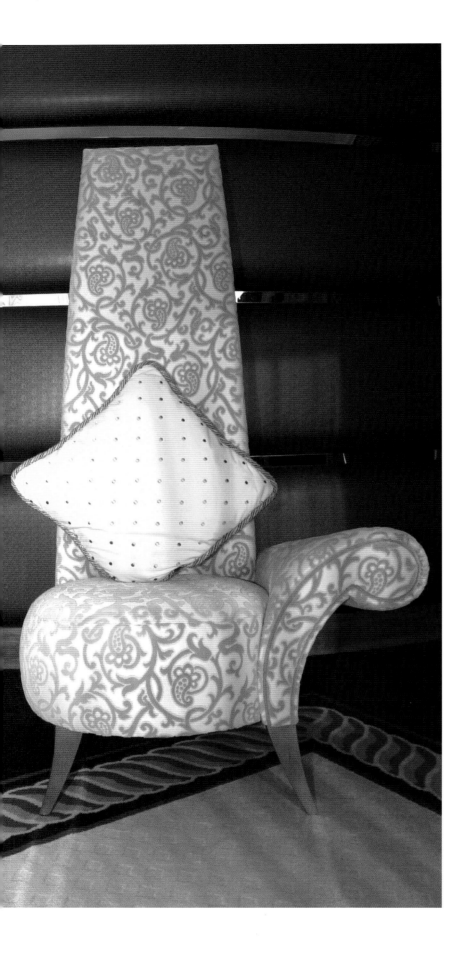

The lavish finishes of leather, silks and velvets conceal discreetly the high-tech amenities in each and every Suite. A 24 hour butler service for all Suites is standard. Checking into the hotel means checking in in the privacy of your Suite. Your butler will unpack your suitcase, and guide you through on how to work your Door intercom and video camera display on your 54" plasma screen Digital TV (with over 70 channels) and surround sound Home Theatre system, the DVD player, the motorised drapes and video conferencing etc. - all from a 'gameboy' style touch screen controller for the room entertainment and information systems.

In the Study, the Toshiba notebook Laptop computer is standard issue (if you want to excess the rest of the world on Internet) together with your Fax Machine and Printer.

In every room of every Suite is a separate Lighting Scene Dimmer System, a 'ghost' clock (light projected) in the hallway and the mirror on the ceiling above your bed, a great topic of conversation. Every suite has its own fully serviced Bar and counter, with a minibar also in the bedroom and minimum 9 telephones in each Suite.

The Suites range from a mere 1 Bedroom Suite of 169 sq. metres to the 2 Grand Suites of 780 sq. metres each, both covering the entire top floor of the Burj Al Arab.

ROYAL SUITE

The Royal Suites, of which there are a pair, cover the entire 25th floor of the Burj Al Arab. This is the ultimate in luxury in the interior of the Burj Al Arab.

Each Royal Suite, with the advantage of its own private elevator is on 2 levels linked also by a very grand staircase in the Entrance Lobby. A royal yellow floor trimmed in a black and white glass mosaics invite you into a series of majestic rooms covering a total area of 780 sq. metres. The sun-burst theme and fiery sun colours runs throughout.

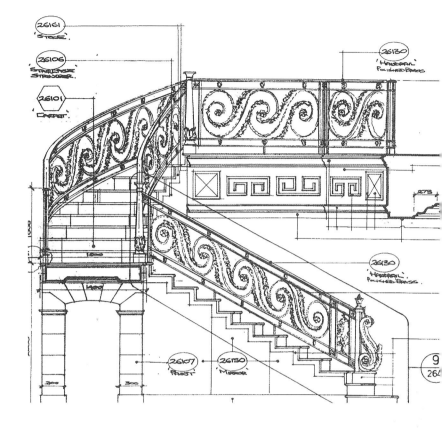

The Study, which converts also into a guest bedroom, is fitted with a private collection of books and videos, all leather bound and as in all rooms in the Royal Suite, meticulously selected artifacts decorate each corner.

The Drawing Room is adorned with the richest of silks, 24 carat gilt mouldings, a Japanese lacquer and gold screen, crystal chandelier and the thickest hand tufted wool carpets. The formal room to receive the most important guest and VIP.

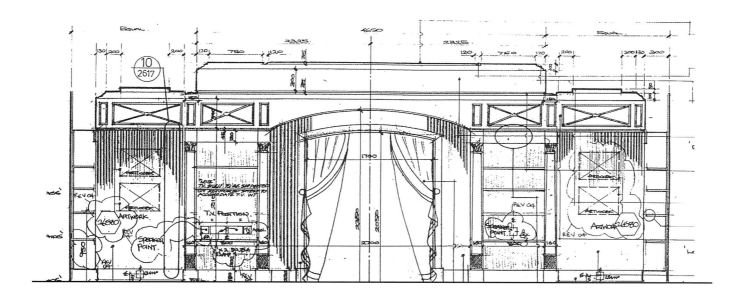

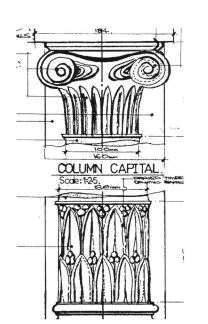

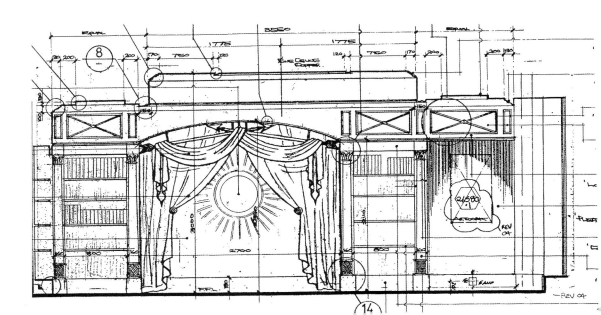

COLUMN CAPITAL
Scale: 1:25

9 COLUMN CAPITAL.
— Not To Scale.

The Royal Suite has its own Private Cinema for a comfortable seating of 12 persons.

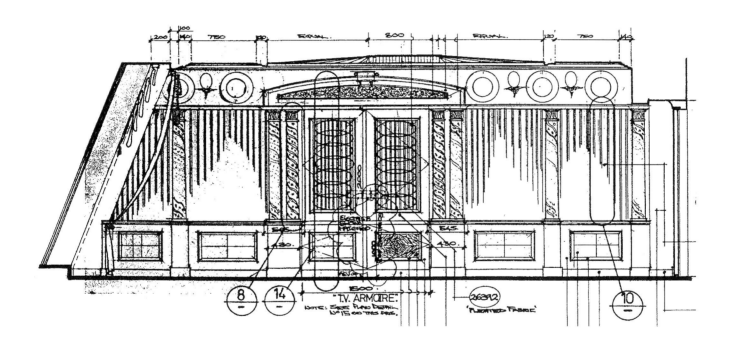

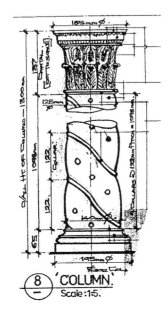

8 'COLUMN'.
— Scale: 1:5.

The Dining room is the essence of the sunburst theme with the carpetmotive reflected in the sky coffer in the ceiling and the colours inspired by the reds and yellows on the sun.

The Upper Level of the Royal Suite has another Sitting Room, often referred to as the Ladies Sitting Room, with a Majlis style seating covered in leopard velvet upholstery, with its own plasma screen TV. The ceiling coffer is tented in silk, Arabic style.

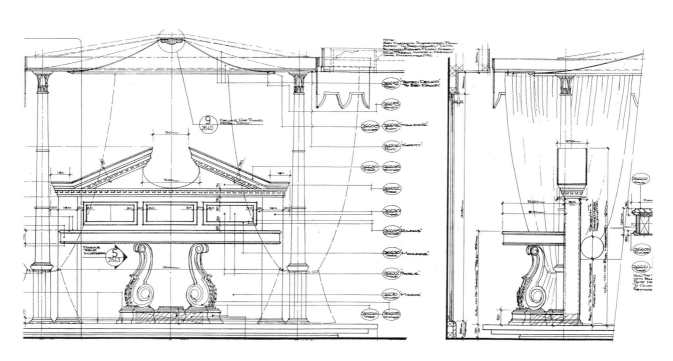

There are 2 Grand Bedrooms with its own Bathrooms.

The Master Bedroom has a revolving Bed fit for a King. En Suite Bathrooms are palatial proportions finished in hand tufted carpets sunk in around marble and mosaic borders. Gold bathroom accessories, gilt cornices, hand painted murals, cover every square inch of these amazingly rich areas.

The Second Master Bedroom is the more feminine of the two Bedrooms, with its more refined and paler colours.

The adjoining bathroom has the rare Fantastico Arni marble obtained (with great difficulty) from a quarry that was closed 50 years ago.

BEHIND THE SCENES . . . . .

ARCHITECTURE ENGINEERING & CONSTRUCTION MANAGEMENT

WS ATKINS & PARTNERS OVERSEAS

For the Jumeirah Beach Resort development (Burj Al Arab, Wild Wadi, Jumeirah Beach Hotel, Al Maha Villas, Conference Centre), WS Atkins & Partners were the lead consultant to have provided master planning, architecture, engineering and cost and construction management. Well established in Dubai for many years prior to this project, WS Atkins & Partners mobilised a completely self-sufficient and fully resourced design and construction management office on the construction site, 140 strong at its peak.

A design statement on the Burj Al Arab from **Tom Wright**, Design Director of WS Atkins Architecture:

"I was hoping you might be able to pop over to Dubai, I think I have something interesting for you to design....."

I replaced the receiver and looked out the window at the rain. Barry Chapman, the Dubai office MD, not known for sponsoring architects to go anywhere, was offering me an all expenses paid holiday in the sun. The tallest hotel in the world? Sounded like another unfeasible idea that would never see the light of day, but who was I to argue. It was October 1993.

We went straight from the airport to a meeting with the client's representative who confirmed that the wave-shaped hotel that had previously been shown to the client was liked and that we now had two weeks to come up with designs for an all suite tower hotel.

The tower was to become an icon for the developing Dubai, as Sydney has its opera house and Paris the Eiffel Tower, so Dubai was to have a similar landmark.

It was soon realised that to create a building that would become iconic was the most difficult aspect of the conceptual design. A list was drawn up of instantly recognisable buildings that had become synonymous with a city or country.

The prerequisite of the list was if the form of the building could be drawn and recognised within 10 seconds, Pictorial style. The list was surprisingly small and most of the buildings were historical. Try it for yourself, you will be lucky to find 10 buildings in the world that fall

within the category. You will find that each of the buildings has one thing in common, an ecnomy and uniqueness of form.

It was also suggested that the tower was to represent the culture of Dubai. This immediately posed a problem as I had no knowledge of the history of the people and had even found myself looking at the map in the in-flight magazine to locate Dubai on planet Earth. The first week was therefore spent exploring. We found that the money from oil had been used to fuel the redevelopment of the city. The modern buildings that decimated the old town with its traditional wind towers, save a few, are mostly 'fast food architecture' thrown up to provide office accommodation and housing for the expatriate workers who temporarily flock to Dubai for a slice of the action. It didn't take long to realise that the people of Dubai were enjoying their newly found freedom and wanted to be seen as a fast developing forward looking "first world" culture. This being the case we decided to look at the future aspirations of the people for our ideas rather than basing them on the limited historical cultural context.

Dubai sees itself as modern, stylish and forward thinking. A holiday destination, "the leisure, shopping sporting capital of the Arabian gulf". We were seeking an image that was evocative, recognisable, and expressed these desires. The Arabian Gulf had always been a major focus for the city and now with the fast emerging tourist trade reinforcing the maritime association it seemed reasonable to design the tower hotel in the form of a giant sail. Not the shape of the historic dhow but the shape of a modern high tech sail, the type of sail that would be found on a yacht in St. Tropez.

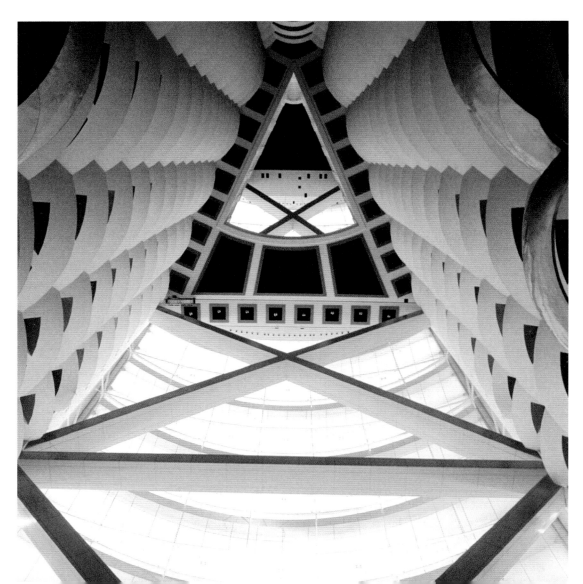

The type of sail that has always evoked a sense of luxury, excitement, sophistication and adventure. To complete the design, we would build the sail on an island offshore creating a building that we hoped would instantly be recognisable the world over.

Two weeks were up and we had ten tower schemes and a model of our favourite choice, the sail. As the presentation drew to a close the client pronounced that the sail would be built, starting tomorrow.

Slightly stunned, Chapman and I walked out. "You know," he said, "I think he was serious!"

The rest is history.

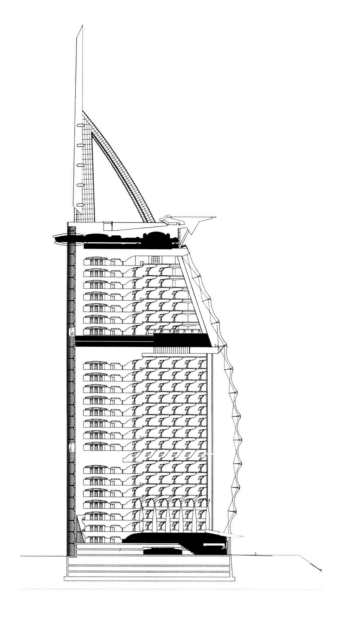

MAIN CONSTRUCTION

AL HABTOOR
MURRAY & ROBERTS

The Al Habtoor Murray & Roberts partnership commenced in earnest early 1995 when they joined hands to tender on one of the world's most challenging and prestigious construction contracts, the Burj Al Arab hotel main superstructure.

Al Habtoor Murray & Roberts is proud to be associated with this magnificent project. Not only were they responsible for the main superstructure which included the supply and erection of the structural steelwork from Murray & Roberts Group Company in South Africa, Al Habtoor Murray & Roberts were also contracted to fit-out all the back of house facilities and all the luxurious suites, reaching incomparable standards never been seen before with the quality of finishes ranging from rare marble and granite, murals designed with glass mosaics, to intricate inlay joinery work and gold leafing. The diversity of disciplines within the Al Habtoor Murray & Roberts organisation is immense.

Sept. 96: LIMITED ACCESS / CRANAGE / FORMWORK
Limited accessibility to manmade island 300m offshore via temporary
construction bridge. 3-tower cranes, largest ever in the Middle East. (76t metre capacity)

The pictorial insight to some of the major challenges faced during construction from April 1996 to November 1999, provides an indication of the extent of professional expertise in the mastery of engineering, construction, and detail finishing.

A fine example of an international and a local company working together successfully on one of the most outstanding projects in Dubai and the world.

Nov. 96: ATRIUM TAKES SHAPE
The world's tallest atrium beginning to take shape.
First sections of rear bracing steelwork in position.

Feb. 97: "WINTER" WINDS
Strong winds restricting all lifting operations -
External steelwork erection gaining momentum.

April 97: HEAVIEST LIFT
Centre diagonal weighing
165t positioned for lifting
with strand jacks.

July 97: CONCRETE TOP OUT SCAFFOLDING TO THE HEAVENS
12 months for 56 floors · End suites steelwork on climbing · First signs of interior suite facades

Notable Data:

Total Height:	321 metres
Concrete:	60,000 cubic metres
Reinforcing steel:	9,000 t
Structural Steelwork:	9,000 t
Cladding:	80,000 square metres
Fabric sail wall:	10,000 square metres of double skin PTFE coated glass fibre
Exoskeleton Frame:	273 metres high (equivalent to a 78 storey building)
Diagonals:	6 x triangular pipe bracings largest is 85metres long (165 t)
Mast:	104 metres long
Helipad:	330 t steel structure supported on 1 metre diameter x 50 mm thick steel pipes.
Skyview Restaurant:	1000 sq. metres Floor Area, 350t Steel, Cantilevered 26 m from the face of the building, 200m above sea level.

Nov. 97:
4-TOWER CRANES
· Sail wall supports in position
· Exoskeleton keeps on climbing
· 4 tower cranes

Nov. 97: NIGHTSHIFT
Sunset in the Gulf and nightshift rises on the island.

Dec. 97: "FISH" EYEVIEW
Fish eyeview of helipad under construction
Sail walls ready to drop
Curtain wall / cladding takes shape.

April 98: SAIL WALL
Sail wall positioned (Another world's largest)

June 98: "FALCONS'S" EYEVIEW
Falcon's eyeview of exoskeleton, skyview restaurant & helipad.

INTERIOR DESIGN

KCA International Designers

Our story from **Khuan Chew**, Design Principal of KCA International:

Sitting in our office in April 1995, the call came informing us that KCA International had been 1 of 16 companies shortlisted for the competition of interiors to 2 hotels in the Chicago Beach Resort Development in Dubai. We were visited by a representative from the development the next day and were provided with drawings and pre-requisite information. Is this for real, we asked each other? Whilst we had worked on mega projects before (as employees of big practices), this one looked unbelievably humungus. Perhaps another "pie in the sky" we thought (we were quite used to quoting on 'dream projects' and 9 out of 10 times they remained 'dream projects').

The conditions for participation in the competition were to provide a minimum of 1 scheme for the Typical Guestroom of either the Resort Hotel (now the Jumeirah Beach Hotel) or a Typical suite for the Tower Hotel (now the Burj Al Arab) or both (if you were feeling

generous or could work at 1000 mph), in 10 days (Presentation in Dubai on 24th April 1995).

Our starting point was to gather as much information on Dubai, the Emirates, Arabic history and culture, Arabic Sciences and Arts ...literally anything we could find in London.

I had never set foot in Dubai before except for a refuelling stopover when I was 14 en route to school in England. We spent 3 days collating the information, 2 days absorbing it (or trying to) and panicked on the 6th day! There was a wealth of information and references to draw from. Finally we decided on the natural elements of Fire Water Earth and Air.

These natural elements were necessary for the Arabic people to respect for their survival in such harsh terrain and they were close to Allah.

It also lent itself well to work with the dramatic and futuristic architecture of WS Atkins. The drama of the architecture had to be complemented.

After a heavy brainstorming session of 4 days, and feeling rather confident, I took off for sunny Dubai. Upon arrival I bumped into my other competitors and was quite in awe when I soon realised that they were all from the "premiere league" in the design world !! All eight companies (it had dwindled down from 16 by then) went through a "crit" interview one after the other, to the engineers, the architects, the project managers, and the client's representative. We were then given 2 hours to set up our wares in the Function Room in a 4 sq. metre cubicle allocated to each participant. "Be back at 9 pm" ready to present to the Client, and you will only be given 10 minutes maximum. On the dot, he arrived. I was 4th in tow. Bad number (by oriental superstition) I thought. Never mind, Khuan, with all these big companies presenting their stuff with gilt frames, black velvet draped over their work, crystal glasses and even soap to match with hotel logo and all (I only had my pencil sketches, books of references and a couple of boards showing my theme of Arabic Sciences, Astrology, and the Elements), tomorrow you can enjoy lying on the beach when this is all over !!!

When my turn came, the Client apparently gave me 25 minutes, but I only remember that he asked a lot of questions and showed interest in my themes, especially the four elements, and he was quite politely intrigued with my books! Phew!

Promptly after he left, the results were known. 2 parties were singled out in our waiting room next door, one for the Tower (Burj Al Arab), and KCA for the Resort (Jumeirah Beach Hotel). I kissed the sunny beach goodby and had to report for work 8 am sharp!!

The best was yet to come.

2 years on, 15 trips later (well seasoned traveller to Dubai by then) and 2 months before the opening of the Jumeirah Beach Hotel, that other auspicious call came. Would we like to participate in the design competition for the Tower Hotel (Burj Al Arab). Come again? At this eleventh hour? You can't be serious? Yes they were. But surely, I won't have a chance, after all, the Client is a fair man, and I have already the Resort hotel under my belt, he is not going to give the big one to me?! The message came back loud and clear - don't you dare refuse participation in the competition. Of course not! I wouldn't dream of turning it down.

1 week to come up with a scheme for a typical suite for the Burj Al Arab. No problem. And having met the Client on quite a few occasions before for the Resort, I was sure I understood his brief better than ever before. But the brief was very different. Brighter, more adventurous, very outrageous and extravagant. Comb the world for any extraordinary product or finish. We won.....again! It had been an epic journey to get here, and now all we had left to do was design the entire interior of the tallest, most opulent hotel in the world. Our design programme was a record 10 months, issuing over 800 drawings, specification files of 80 different fabric sources, 28 lighting manufactrers, 67 furniture companies.....etc.

I get the feeling the "premiere league" just got some new players.

INTERIOR CONSTRUCTION
& FITTING-OUT (Public Areas)

DEPA INTERIORS
& ARABTEC HOTEL INTERIORS

Depa Interiors & Arabtec Hotel Interiors, executed the interior fitting out of all the public areas in the Burj Al Arab.

Their domain stretch beyond Dubai to the rest of the Middle East, into North Africa, Europe, America and Asia. This global network allows their clients to benefit from the experience, knowledge, organisational ability, purchasing power and facilities they provide, all necessary for the fitting out of the complex public areas of the Burj Al Arab.

Depa/Arabtec was also the contractor for the interiors of the Jumeirah Beach Hotel which opened in 1997, and in November 1998 were appointed on the Burj Al Arab.

The diversity and vitality of the company can be seen in the high quality of the interior of the Burj Al Arab, from stone and marble work to intricate glass mosaic installation, complex joinery inlay to contoured highly polished brass finishes, thousands of sheets of gold and silver leafing to GRG and GRP structures. Their skilled artisans from their various factories supported the Dubai outfit to realise this monumental project .

The Al Iwan Restaurant is a fine example of specialist craftsmenship in the intricate 3 dimensional relief wood carvings and gold leafing to decorative panels and Arabic arches executed with perfection by Depa/ Arabtec.

Every public area called for contrasting styles of designs and decoration. Hundreds of finishes and products were sourced, procured and installed - as can be seen here in the Juna Bar, the Al Falak Ballroom, the Atrium and the Assawan Spa Health Club.

SPECIALIST PRODUCTS
(GRP & GRC)

ARABIAN PROFILE CO. LTD.
(a subsidiary company of GIBCA)

The design of the interior architecture called for unconventional materials and highly specialised structures which required high performance products to be fabricated.

Established in 1984, the Arabian Profile Co. Ltd. (APL) a leading Emirates manufacturer of sheet-metal products, glass-fibre reinforced polyester (GRP) and glassfibre concrete (GRC), was appointed on the Burj Al Arab. Their reputation, knowledge, experience and innovative thinking in this highly specialised field allowed the Architectural and Design Consultants a freedom of design to express their creativity to the extreme.

Hence, the successful results as evident in the Atrium sail walls (GRP), the mirror finish stainless steel balcony fascia in the 3 lower Atrium floors, the VIP Entrance, and the complicated structures of the Water Cascade and Fountain also in the Atrium.

APL's contribution also extended to the aerodynamic roof structure for the "Fin - Expression" in the Swimming Pool area of the Bab Al Yam; and the glass-fibre reinforced polyester structure covering the support concrete structure of the main bridge.

Notable Data:

Sail Wall :

3mm GRP (fire retarded) 1 hour fire rating 25mm Polypropylene FR Honeycomb Largest GRP construction (m2) 110 m2 ever awarded. Each panel weighs 3.5 tons. Each Panel load bearing structure and Fire Wall.

Atrium Water Features:

A perfect GRP/Honeycomb horizontal structure made up of indiviual trays or segmented elements bolted together on site allowing adjustments of horizontal levels.

Roof Structure (Pool):

An Aerodynamic 700 m2 "FinExpression" roof structure. Standing Seam Aluminium Panels, edge coated with GEL coat finish. Secondary ceiling in timber laminate with epoxy saturated veneer skin laminated to a honeycomb structure. Weather proof to extreme humidity, heat and salt spray. Each panel weigh only 5.5kg/m2.

Bridge Cover:

GRP structure is mounted by return flanges internally and hung to support main concrete structure. The panels are load bearing and spans from both edges of the bridge to the centre line covering all Mechanical, Electrical, and Plumbing and all other installations in a complete water tight "duct."

WS Atkins
Woodcote Grove
Ashley Road
Epsom
Surrey KT18 5BW
United Kingdom
Tel: +44 1372 726 140
Fax: +44 1372 740 055

Al Habtoor Murray & Roberts
Joint Venture
16th Floor
Al Moosa Tower
Sheikh Zayed Road
P.O. Box 30023
Dubai
U.A.E.
Tel: +9714 331 3826
Fax: +9714 331 7523

KCA International
111 Westminster Business Square
Durham Street
London SE11 5JH
United Kingdom
Tel: +44 20 7582 8898
Fax: +44 20 7582 8860

Arabtec Depa Hotel Interiors
Al Reem Tower
18th Floor
Al Maktoum Street
P.O.Box 56338
Dubai
U.A.E.
Tel: +9714 224 3800
Fax: +9714 224 3700

Arabian Profile Co. Ltd.
P.O. Box 3195
Sharjah
U.A.E.
Tel: +9716 533 2624
Fax: +9716 533 2334

ACKNOWLEDGEMENTS

Hundreds of companies (suppliers and contractors) participated in the making of the Burj Al Arab, many of them provided information and images.

It would have been virtually impossible for this book to materialise without the support and encouragement of many fellow consultants and contractors on the Burj Al Arab project namely WS Atkins, Al Habtoor Murray & Roberts, DEPA Arabtec and Arabian Profile Co. Ltd. I thank them for their tremendous support.

We owe thanks also to many colleagues and friends for their advice and patience during the preparation of this very ambitious project, especially Colin Ash and Kate Carolan, with their masterly command of the English Language, and John Carolan, for his persistent diplomacy in the chase for relevant information from various sources, and Sheikh Sultan bin Saqr Al Qassimi, whose good humour, enthusiasm and belief in our capability on this project spurred us on.

Special thanks to the main contributors of visual material and information: Tom Wright and his team at WS Atkins (Eleanor Smith tirelessly forwarding HR scans on CD), Mohannad Sweid of DEPA Arabtec, for his genuine willingness in offering hundreds of images from his archives, and Gillian Best Powell who spent countless hours sifting through these archives with us, Malcolm Murphy of Al Habtoor Murray & Roberts with his invaluable pictures during every stage of construction, Domus Tiles Ltd. and Polaron Controls Ltd.

Thanks to also numerous amateur photographers, many who worked during the construction of the Burj Al Arab.

A special mention and credit to Charles Crowell (photographer for Depa Arabtec) and to Jumeirah International who offered many images and information from their marketing department and library.

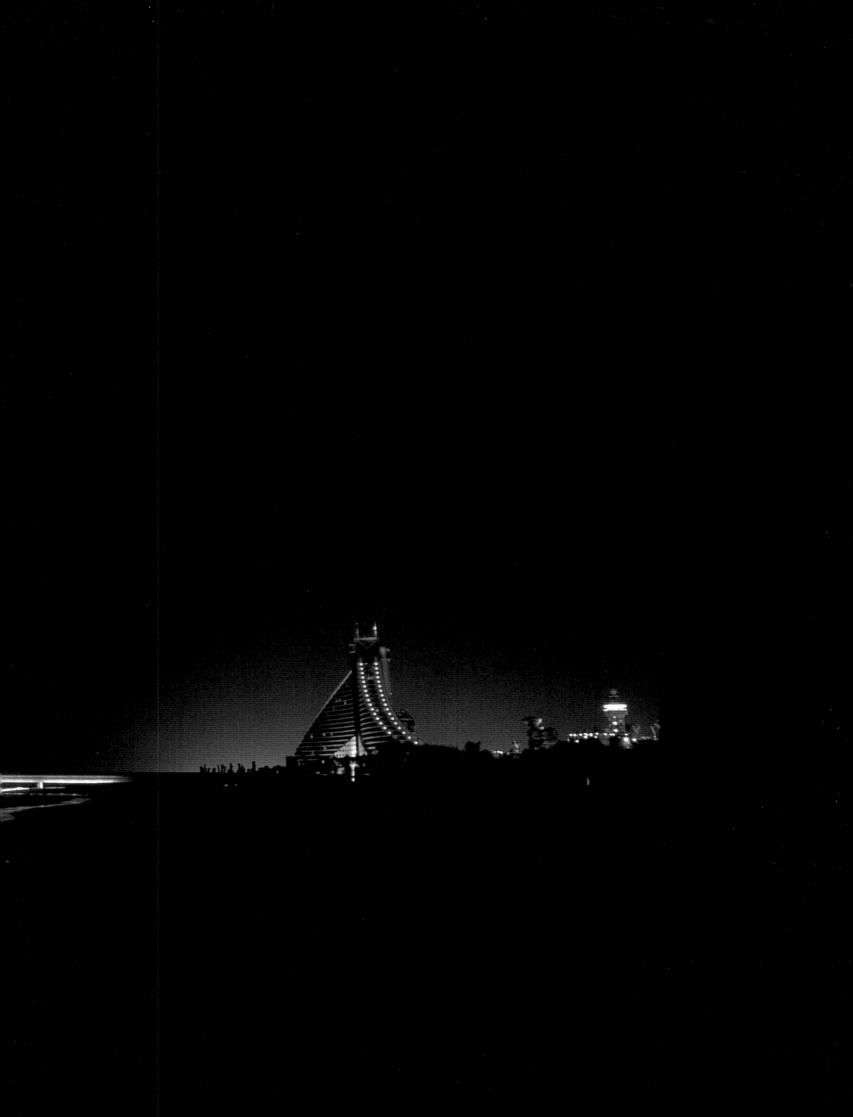

BURJ AL ARAB VITAL STATISTICS

Construction sequence of the island:

230 Number of steel piles
Length of piles 45 m
Diameter of piles 1.5 m
Depth of lowest basement (B3) under sea is
5000 m below DMD (Dubai Mean Datum) i.e.
7000 m below sea level.

Heights:

15th tallest building in the world
Taller than the Eiffel Tower
Height of atrium 182 m
Height of helipad from sea 212 m
Height of top accommodation from island, 27th
floor (Al Muntaha "Skyview" Restaurant) is
197.5 m above DMD.
The island is 7.5 m above DMD. Therefore the
Al Muntaha is 190 m above the top of
the island.
Height of top of mast from island 321 m.
Length of mast 60 m
Exoskeleton Frame 273 m high

Dimensions:

Distance of building off shore 450 m to the outer
point of the island 270 m off shore.
Size of island 150 m per side
Sea 7.5 m deep
SHED hollow armour units surround the island
Length of biggest truss 85 m
Weight of biggest truss 165 t
Cantilever of sky view restaurant 27 m
& 1.7 m deep
Helipad is 330 t steel structure supported on 1 m
diameter x 50 mm thick steel pipes
Weight of helicopter that can land on
helipad 7.5 tonnes
Maximum sway at top of
accommodation 300 mm
50 year wind record is 34 mps/mph
Total volume of concrete on island 60,000 sq.m
Total tonnage of steel 9,200 tonnes
Gross Area of building 120,000 sq.m
28 double height floors 7 m floor to floor
Atrium volume 285,000 cm
Area of fabric wall, 10,000 sq.m x 2
Width of fabric up to 50 m
Thickness of fabric 1 mm with
500 mm air gap
Number of fabric trusses 12, not
including level 26. Hung by cables from
18th & 26th floors
Diameter of cables 52 mm
Total length of cables 1km

GRG Sail Wall 35,000 sq.m
Aquariums in Atrium hold 250,000 litres
of water
Al Mahara Aquarium holds 280,000 litres
of water

Construction Data:

Number of large cranes used 3
Maximum load of cranes 760 mt
Number of Design Team on site (Architects,
Engineers, Construction Managers, Interior
Designers) over 160
4,000 construction staff on site at peak
How many man years to construct
(i.e. how long for one man alone in years)
8,000 years (poor old chap)
350 man years to design and construction
manage

Special Equipment and Data:

Lifts:
Service   4 m per sec (9 mph)
Wall Climber   5 m per sec (11 mph)
Passenger   7 m per sec (16 mph)
Control plates of lighting integrated with control
of air conditioning system in all suites.
Control systems of over 20,000 channels
of lighting and dimming.

Guest Amenities:

142   1 Bedroom Suites (169 sq.m)
18   1 Bedroom End Suites (315 sq.m)
4   1 Bedroom Deluxe Suites (330 sq.m)
28   2 Bedroom Suites (335 sq.m)
6   3 Bedroom Suites (670 sq.m)
2   Presidential Suites (667 sq.m)
2   Royal Suites (780 sq.m)

Food & Beverage Outlets & Public Areas:

Al Muntaha (Skyview) 27th Floor seats 120,
bar lounge seats 74
Al Mahara (Undersea) seats 114
Al Iwan (1st Floor) seats 110
Sahn Eddar (Atrium) seats 120
Bab Al Yam (Poolside) seats 84
Juna Bar (Mezzanine) seats 35
Assawan Spa Lounge seats 50
Diwania (Library) seats 26
Al Falak Ballroom seats 230
(theatre seats 350)
Suheil Conference Room seats 16
Suha Conference Room seats 30
Athuraya Conference seats 30